"*first you must destroy the world* collects **poetry of 'hedonist reach' and thirst, laid down in what the poet understands to be the too small fields of little deaths**, where 'flesh surrender as good/as any peace treaty' won't drown out the big deaths, those wars outside the poet's windows and inside her own history. Just as firmly, she holds that people needed to make people before wars could take them, and so **Claudia Saleeby Savage's poems do not keep time with Eros** *despite* **Ares,** rather as anti-weapon, *as a frequent condition of life, as one means 'to bring up the water of the other.'* Tears, here, are for loss of life, memory, and connection, for Syria, for touch that could be sensual but is instead brutal. This collection grips that tension in remarkable lines of musicality and invention, frank desire, with imagery that stuns and dazzles."

—**DOUGLAS KEARNEY**, AUTHOR OF *I IMAGINE I BEEN SCIENCE FICTION ALWAYS, SHO* & *OPTIC SUBWOOF*

"Claudia Saleeby Savage's *first you must destroy the world* is raw grit and power. It is **an awakening of our senses beyond the material world, a recollection of what it means to be human**. Reading these poems, I was left breathless and humbled at the many ramifications and repercussions of war. ***These poems will not let us forget family, place, or loss.*** They will not let us forget each other or leave anyone behind. They are a call to remember our humanity in all its hurt, in all its sweetness, in all its anger and sorrow. Thank you, Claudia, for this collection—for reminding us we are not immune; for reminding us of what we pick up in the worlds left behind."

—**ANA-MAURINE LARA**, AUTHOR OF *KOHNJEHR WOMAN* & *ERZULIE'S SKIRT*

"In this unflinching collection, Saleeby Savage confronts the most recent decade of atrocities and breaks open her own heart to ask what she—the mother, the wife, the grandchild of refugees, the poet—can do in the face of overwhelming helplessness and rage. **She puts everything she has in these poems. Like a jazz virtuoso**, she riffs urgently between authoritarian war, erotic joy, state-sponsored starvation, the dark ocean, and her grandmother's plate of lamb and yogurt. *In the face of relentless devastation, Saleeby Savage reminds us that poetry is the anti-weapon, that children are still playing on top of the rubble, and there's a word for hope in every language.*"

—**ARMIN TOLENTINO**, AUTHOR OF *WE MEANT TO BRING IT HOME ALIVE*

"Claudia Saleeby Savage's poems sing. They sing into the parched throat of a lover 'to bring up the water of the other.' They sing into sorrow because 'Love is already too brief.' They sing into the complexities of identity when the poet admits, 'I am uncomfortable with my own face. My rage sparks daily.' *Perhaps most importantly, these poems sing across borders because there is 'Always a border somewhere & those intent on crossing.'* With exhilarating lyric intensity, Savage's poems sing the horrors and pleasures of life in the 21st century."

—**ROB SCHLEGEL**, AUTHOR OF *CHILDCARE*

"From the first poem of Claudia Saleeby Savage's new book, *first you must destroy the world*, you are aiming for the last line—"the poet takes whatever is left/and breathes it back alive." **What is lost, and what must be recovered, sifts through the poet's hands like water—family lineages salvaged from Syrian rubble and refugee rafts, including her own sitti's stories that survived the years**: 'Always a border somewhere & those intent on crossing. / The streets heave iron. This place wants to send them back. She misses sand. / She misses foam.' This wide and sensual collection is a musical notation of erasure. *Savage conjures the sounds of missing in both empty swaths and staccato on the page—the symbols we are told stand in for the sound of a mother sshhing, or the sound a missile makes through the air on its way to its target*: 'tip your child's head up/hope their hearts/turn to wonder=====.' Savage brings her fully awake, desirous, and protective self to each poem, accepting the weight of the task to tell any story of the unclaimed and the unnamed: 'you will not / be just a / thumb drive. / your husband's comb. your daughter's medicine. a drawing by your grandfather. / a handful of dirt. / a piece of Syria / hold it close.' Reading Savage's poems, at this moment when we are, as a nation, choosing how close to hold each other, the stranger amongst us, is to confront the question 'what matters when the moon shrivels you/...do you know your neighbors?' She reminds us that *even while we are lost in grief, we are charged with un-erasing history and shining a merciful light on the retelling*. The poet knows destroying and re-claiming the world are the two sides of the heart's fragile coin."

—**KRISTIN BERGER**, AUTHOR OF *ECHOLOCATION* & *HOW LIGHT REACHES US*

"Born during the Syrian thirteen-year-long civil war and refugee crisis, the stunning poems collected in *first you must destroy the world*, fuse the personal and the political like no other poems I know. To say these are poems of empathy would not be quite right, because empathy does not go far enough. Not for the poet who insists on conjuring away map lines—between self and other, us and them, citizen and refugee, body and spirit—until they make new and dazzling patterns on the page. Not for the poet who, in conversation with her ancestral ghosts, can trace the twisting double helixes of ancestral lines until we have to ask, 'when did here become here?' ***No matter how fractured and broken by violence or grief, this poet breathes the shards back to life and into a fierce and irresistible music. These are poems that stay up all night dancing and wailing with grief, but they also draw you into the most tender intimacies.*** You will not be able to sit still, you will not be able to look away, and if you do, those refugees who kept moving as you made your way through these pages, moving in the interstices between poems, between the silences, who must decide what to take when they must leave everything behind, they will follow you. If you are feeling numbed by the daily horror of headlines, this book is the elixir that will quicken your deepest humanity."

—**ALEXIS LATHEM**, AUTHOR OF *LAMBS IN WINTER* & *ALPHABET OF BONES*

FIRSTMATTERPRESS

Portland, Ore.

first you must destroy the world

first you must destroy the world

claudia saleeby savage

FIRSTMATTERPRESS

Portland, Ore.

First Edition

Published in the United States
by First Matter Press
Portland, Oregon

Paperback ISBN-13: 978-1-958600-13-9
Library of Congress Control Number: 2025945019

Editor: Lauren Paredes
Contributing Editors: ash good, Emily Moon & Hailey Spencer
In Cohort: nawa angel a.h., Annemarie Eayrs & Violeta Garza
Contributing Readers: Sonya Wohletz & Andra Vltavín
Copy Editor: Andra Vltavín

Cover: *Grays Harbor*
5 inches x 7 inches (monotype)
Copyright © 2025 by Pearlyn Tan
pearlyn.net

Book design by ash good
ashgood.com

This project was made possible by Regional Arts and Culture Council,
Multnomah County Cultural Coalition and Oregon Cultural Trust.

FIRSTMATTERPRESS.ORG

for my daughter

POEMS

NOTE

*The symbol ======= should be verbalized
as a "shhh" sound, such as a snake in a tunnel
or a bomb cutting the sky on the way to its target.*

i cannot afford sleep
—Wanda Coleman

slip of light

a rithā' for Abdullah Kurdi

for a moment before you hit the water

before you hit the water

before your father reached for   the water

before the water   you checked your pocket for your stuffed bird

its turquoise wings safe and warm inside your coat   before you and your

pocketed bird flew   through a low cloud   before you hit the water

you and your pocketed bird flew

your father, your mother, your brother   took flight

near you   you didn't know your father scooped water

before you hit   he scooped water   held the larger liquid

the dark, black water   the body liquid, thinking

it was you

did he whisper *shhh, shhh* in your ear before you hit the water

his breath the shape of waves

the sky, the clouds, the mist, melting   water

between your fingers   water on water, water to water   which way

to water   with you in his arms   your mother beside him

your brother in front, near

did it seem   before, at first, for a moment   an adventure

real and imagined merging as water   as mist   as cloud

the land behind you lit and red,   your heart   the same burn

and, your brother, only 2 years older, in on the lie

the story that your house would stay   the door a cradling mouth

your bed   a blanket of pale-yellow   embroidered suns saving your body's

small sigh

quick quick, the sea will take us to Greece your father's hands a boat

for your stuffed bird, up and down   up and down till you smiled

your mother's face   another sea   wet with salt   *look,* she pointed to the water

she fussed   soft bangs from your eye

your father's arms crushed your ribs   you in the boat, then, your brother

then, your mother   tiny boat   too many, two dozen in the boat, before

your mother's chest heaving   your brother gripping the hull

each knuckle a small white moon

the dark confusing

                        sea for sky   waves thick in your ears

waves together   water   wind   and wind,   and wind

your father unsure   hold the boat?   swim?   where was your brother?

        where   your mother?   where?

                                    where   where

are you   ?

the sea is greedy   belly fat on whale   and jellyfish   porpoise   sardine

garbage continents drift   kelp cities   still it belches ships

dolphin bone corral   marooned bear

how to explain the smallness of a 3-year-old's lungs

        an apple, split   a ripe fig after the wasp's retreat

                                    the air's defeat to the push of

                        water

and then   the brother

        and then, the mother

how to explain a father forced   to shore

      in the dark   alone   arms

so heavy he doesn't know how

      just before   the waves   just before

                the water, just before   the water

he sang to the waves, he sang to everything   just before

everything, everything

      to the waves   the water   everything   the water

in his hands   through his hands

                     water   empty of light

=======

take something with you, anything, to remember you are you, you will not be just a number. your wedding sheets. your cat. your mother's gold necklace. your grandmother's diamond ring. wooden spoons. blue bowl. tea pot. coffee pot. embroidered pillowcases. your daughter's bird blanket. your son's stuffed elephant. socks. pants. grandpa's medicine. your son's inhaler. a box of tampons. a book. a copper pot. a pacifier. a lighter. matches. a thumb drive. laptop. printer. monitor. family album. family picture. purse. backpack. flute. cushion. saxophone. drum. baby food. biscuits. water. water. biscuits. sugar packets. water. your father's gold watch. water. your grandmother's ring. your sister's bracelet. water. a box of tampons. a book. your prayer shawl. your prayer blanket. the cat. your son's stuffed elephant. water. pants. grandpa's medicine. your son's inhaler. a pot. cushion. a bag. a backpack. take something with you, anything, to remember you are you. you will not be just a number. your favorite sheets. a hammer. a knife. a thumb drive. your mother's copper coffee pot. your daughter's favorite hair bow. your youngest's silky blanket. hair brush. toothbrush. toothpaste. glasses. soap. soap. soap. socks. pants. grandpa's medicine. your son's inhaler. a box of tampons. a book. a copper pot. a pacifier. a lighter. matches. a thumb drive. laptop. printer. monitor. family album. family picture. purse. backpack. flute. cushion. saxophone. drum. baby food. biscuits. water. water. biscuits. sugar packets. water. pants. grandpa's medicine. your son's inhaler. a pot. cushion. a bag. a backpack. your soul. take something with you, anything, to remember you are you. you will not be just a number. sheets. a hammer. a knife. a thumb drive. your mother's copper coffee pot. your daughter's favorite hair bow. your youngest's blanket. hair brush. toothbrush. toothpaste. glasses. soap. soap. soap. your husband's comb. your daughter's medicine. a drawing by your grandfather. your grandmother's ring. your sister's bracelet. water. a box of tampons. a book. a pacifier. a lighter. matches. a thumb drive. laptop. printer. monitor. family album. family picture. purse. backpack. your prayer shawl. your prayer blanket. the cat. your son's stuffed elephant. a feather. a stick. a handful of dirt. a handful of dirt. a piece of dirt. a crumb of dirt. stuck in your pocket. whatever is stuck in your pocket. whatever is stuck in your pocket. a rock. whatever is stuck in your pocket. whatever is stuck in your pocket. whatever is stuck in your pocket. whatever is stuck in your pocket. a piece of Syria in your pocket. what is stuck in your pocket. hold it close. it will be all you need.

my daughter discovers synchronicity

If you cannot keep that smell of rosemary on your palms. Tea warm

in your morning mug. Or stop your daughter's howl when the soup

bowl tips. Swallow this sorrow and spit out birds. My daughter gulps air

to better voice her throat's vibration. Her belly's taut drum. The contours

of my face mountain under her gaze. Outside a woodpecker searches for

rot in a telephone pole. Her fingers enter the belly button. A world tucked

in worlds tucked in worlds. In mine there are borders of guns. Refusals.

A veil could mean your children starve. Sunlight honeys my daughter's hair

as I sponge the floor. In the other room my husband's jaw works breath

into his horn. Somewhere someone always struggles more. Maybe it is you.

Maybe this year sorrow or anger held your heart under water. The bitter hot

oolong feels necessary to my throat. Same as my girl holding her arms up

when I least want to give. I'll lift her. Inhale her cheek.

Love is already too brief.

sitti learns the word cat

in the back of the classroom on a stool
she stares at letters straight as desks

straight as the hair of the child in front of her
straight as the floor—the letters

blackboard to ceiling no dance in them no wind
no dome for bread or prayer in the letters—

outside the trees surrender leaves to hidden sun
she wonders how an animal makes itself letters

so full of vibration (whiskers out its tail another music)
how can it be held still in stiff letters

rigid on the blackboard as well as in the mouth
the *t* a rude spitting—no sweetness on the tongue

sacrifice

open open mouth breath till I symphony gooey light tongue pulsing stars

liquid night and my feet vibrate like those swifts migrating in fall. their

flocked bodies tension of frantic wings scooping air. your hands reach

everywhere. entangled with the dark I forget my own beginning. did the

swifts try to hold a slice of cloud as they dove into the chimney? a sliver

of sun? mouths open for every last insect on the way down as your mouth

in my mouth deeper deeper me on top pivoting to metronome hips or

am I the piston and the birds God? my pattern predictable around a fixed

point as they cluster in spirals caterpillars windmills. in that moment when

 they cannot figure trajectory just a flurry of energetic beaks colliding is it

like you assuming the role of lathe as you place me on my knees? I'll never

know what it is to enter another just as I'll never know how they picked the

one to be sent out first for the hawk perched on the edge of their nesting

place. who decides sacrifice? and why does this moment mean little death

when all I do is soar?

you think a violin will melt steel

a crowd chants *na'am. na'am. na'am.* Arab-heart glitter. enough hearts together bird. wings to cover the children. feather the dry ground. they sing to stay. their throats. their land. they sing to stay. they stand. flutter wings. lips to this bit of earth. theirs. sound a wind. sound a wind. sound wind. (theirs.) sound a wind. wind.

out, (no) out brief candle.

they named their child Thawra

thick muscle pliant bone we
hollow out the spine in the morning
crack greeting to the sun
while the finches tremble their home awake
unaware of our relationship with forsythia
(there are things we won't let grow)
we horizon a hillside of holly
we tear old lilacs to ribbons
the neighbor's bass holds our bedroom hostage at night—
so you blast your saxophone, naked 6 a.m.
in the backyard ankle-deep in fallen leaves
while they fever-whiskey dream—
according to the chord you choose their bricks may
crumble like 1989 when we heard the wall come down
the radio's hammers pulsing hope—
unlike now, now the news a series of Syrian artillery torture
Filipino flood Puerto Rican flood Miami flood everything from
the White House to Baltimore to California to
our backyard smoking choking fire—

                              you come back inside

to blow the room body swoon vibration lung tune
exhale and unwound before the room contracts the universe
reverse Big Bang

                              boom

morning sex before I check *Al Jazeera*

mothers die. brothers too. mine. & yours. light slants the trees.
swifts call. & swallow all.

                                              awed by mist. (I barely exist.)

     roll over. under the sheet. (heat / find heat.) who said the roof of the
universe begins with the lover's tongue? (stop thinking!) just funk & sweat.

                                              exhale regret. /

                           (once, I thought nothing would touch our
                           touching the moment before we closed the gap
                           I felt silence envelop our heads snake down our
                           torsos led by spit and breath—loneliness
                           sickness death? never! once, I was wrong
                           ((but let's hold that feeling of lovers in a
                           bubble, a pink bubble, the flame of an oil
                           lantern on a street where time holds still))—
                           once, your breath was the only reason to open
                           my lids to the morning light through the
                           frost-laced window I take flight when you wrap
                           a leg around my hip pin my lips to the mattress
                           ((it is always about this)) when we reminisce it
                           will look like skin abandoning covers it will look
                           like blushing crushing whatever idea you had of
                           us—after a week without we clamor we jab at
                           each other's weakness to get at the soft meat
                           under the belly—once, we never made it past

noon without a go—the-two-year-streak-the-
time-of-bliss-the-flood-after-drought-the-feast-
after-famine-the-euphemism-nesting-deep-in-
side-metaphor when you reach for my
salt-tinged neck in the eaves of my spine I still
tremble I still know where my hands end up
your solar plexus as homing pigeon comes to
me as sure as I came to it—we origami—wrist-
knee-thigh-hip-fold toes in a place they could
not anticipate if it happens in the kitchen so
much the better the steam off the meatballs
simmer patient & your back's made sponge to
maneuver my leg higher

softer   triangulate

hinge my hinges)

sitti teaches me Arabic as pastry

Arabs invented mathematics so you triangle
the dough so quickly I dizzy.

I thought everyone ate them. Sweet
fatty lamb and rich pine nuts. Cinnamon
and bitter parsley. Yogurt tang to sweat
the tongue. Your recipes undecipherable
dashes and ribbons across the paper. A dance
in the mouth even before the mouth.

Silent, confident fingers that crease and twirl.

It can't be 30 years, sitti.

How could you go before teaching me
the word for faith, for hope? *February 2021:*
12.4 million Syrians are food insecure.
80% of the displaced are women and children.
Where is your recipe? Numbers I can
understand. 1 tablespoon of cinnamon.
4 cups of milk. Sorrow steals my sleep.
I am not immune. I need handfuls
of surety, pastry commune.

Green parsley bruise the only ache.

sitti knits hats after dinner for people living on the street

in front of the TV. early 1980s.
why are you crying?

buildings pock-marked & smoking.
women veiled. unveiled.

hands up. blood black splatter.
pale sweater heart-shatter.

poetry should be an anti-weapon

you fear the disaster
after the disaster

the tired that comes
after the bombing

comes after the blood comes

after the mother

falls after the father
goes after the moment

when pistil was renamed pistol

your memory a flower

troubled or was it
your arms awakened

by something
other than spring?

sitti learns her left hook

During fights that lasted more than 10 minutes sitti would scream
Anglo-Saxon at my grandfather. He would yell back *Washington Street*.
Tribal lines. From the New York waterfront to the financial district.
Mini-Syria. Lebanon. Egypt. Jordan. Ancestral ghosts mobbed
the tiny apartment.

What did he know of diaspora?   He was from Kansas.

(And who am I to be telling my grandmother's stories?)

Last one alive keeps the history.

and for water they drank rain

root takes reason to fatten

and you are spent on the earth

wilted matter

what matters when the moon shrivels you

with its false light
the buzz of circuits

day in
day out

images flood
the sea of
brain
bone already soup in
soup (shrivel shrivel)
not a wrinkle
of new thought

to help those

next door

never mind   thousands of miles

                                                        away

                                  do you know your neighbors?

                              =========================

assume
the shape of a body as one body of a body's body. one body only.

then ten.
then seventy.
a thousand. a million. 20 million. 50 million. spiraling to bed. (I dance the
spiral for my daughter. pinwheel my arms while my legs and hips circle.
make her laugh. tell her: *imagine spinning into bed.*
imagine spinning with hundreds

                                  into bed. your body piece of a larger

body puzzle. puzzle body. your body puzzled into
another body.)   furious wings. a hundred raisin-sized hearts squeeze a helix
inside a
helix inside a quaking body.

think that   ==============================

sound and fury signify nothing   but air yielding   to din of skin
the color of mammal milk   this night   we right our ears
as they commune with skull   no lull   close eyes
suffering evaporates in snare   spirit stare   not heart, not eyes

(the witches' brew consisted of Jew—the same as: toad / dog / frog / wolf
and I *am* an animal sometimes / always all of us are   swept away by

thunder /
trace light through windows pale as lace
                                            though always

your face your face
an open door to the street)

                    =================================

                                        ==be strong

        don't forgetto   smallheartbounce

freeecho   metronomebounce

remember your wits / wrists

across / through / on top of the
                              back   underbeat

cling to each other   to the wall
                                   the bark of y(our) hearts
furious static of bat-mimic dip and swoon the moon activates   forgive-

ness and crazes our sliver of brain   what does it help   to want to return
to when migration meant damp insect belly in our belly meant rotted log and rain-
tinged wings   we miss the ground   we dive

        the chimney   elliptical madness   a spiral gyration of wing-dusked
desire for old growth instead of high-rise   forgive us for lusting for what is gone

we are here for you to help   and stare   we are phenomena a momentary break
from the screen   our dance frenzied elegance recall that dream of insect copulation

tip your child's head up

                    hope their hearts
                         turn to wonder=============

=============================

do their elbows sprout fennel?

purplethistlebristle

              mouth wide to suck dew   bloom silver

             whale hue

the pull of the tide // I only know

the pull of the tide // tide // tide

                     I only know the pull of the tide

        the pull of the tide // east and west the

                 pull of the tide // the undertow of you

     whale   *you*   *whale* *//* *whale //* *whale*

              you *//*   *wail* *you* *wail*

wail *wail*

wail

you *answer* *//*

wail *//* *for me*

/ sigh /

use tongue to scoop the blue

from inside me hollow

=========================they / you / we / I

make
worlds. tucked in worlds. tucked in worlds tucked in fat floating fervent
moons. forest thick. ripple water tipple. fingers topple steel. close your eyes
to better remember the scent below the dampest hair.

wait. though.

you do not know you wait.

your stomach knows. a dried gourd. a deflated balloon. moonlight unbright. you wait. a beacon of need. though. you do not know you suffer. (your mother's frantic wings tear the air to ribbons. her beak an open arrow. insects sequin her feathers. desperate flutter.)

=================(*yallah yallah*)

in the sudden rush and whirl wind swallows with her breath / I hid my wings

didn't know

didn't / clouds / your eyes / count / the seconds

where's the flash?

count the / seconds / where's the

thunder? / I molt   /   feathers   /   feathers

rapid regrow   / blue

stare

collarbone dare /

/ / /   inhale

I'll take your air / yes /

yes yes yes yes yes yes yes

yes yes yes / your eyes / yes

the collision of awakening /

I leapt toward the wild season / and got

this nest of skin /

I said something like / fell me / I'm a rooted tree or

touch me / friction begets fire or

keep track of randomness

/ /

I'll keep on

on   on   on   ===================   yallah yallah

see
tapestries threading themselves with sunset. lizard tongue ostrich feather
faded horizon. bass downing trees. as drums rebuild hills. trick lick triptych.

lick my wick(ed) stick. bring floods. bring fire ants. breeding
something feeding   something tearing down the sirens. the horns.

the tsunami of elephants flailing sailing.
they / you / we / I

breach borders

land

firm the yolk. temporary nest. (pregnant pause)

permission to rest?

up.   UP.   UP!

DRINK. EAT. SHIT. ON. ON. ON. ON! MOVE! (this is *not* your country.)

shrill the air. (this is not *our* country.) dare to dare.

crumble at the whisper of a firefly

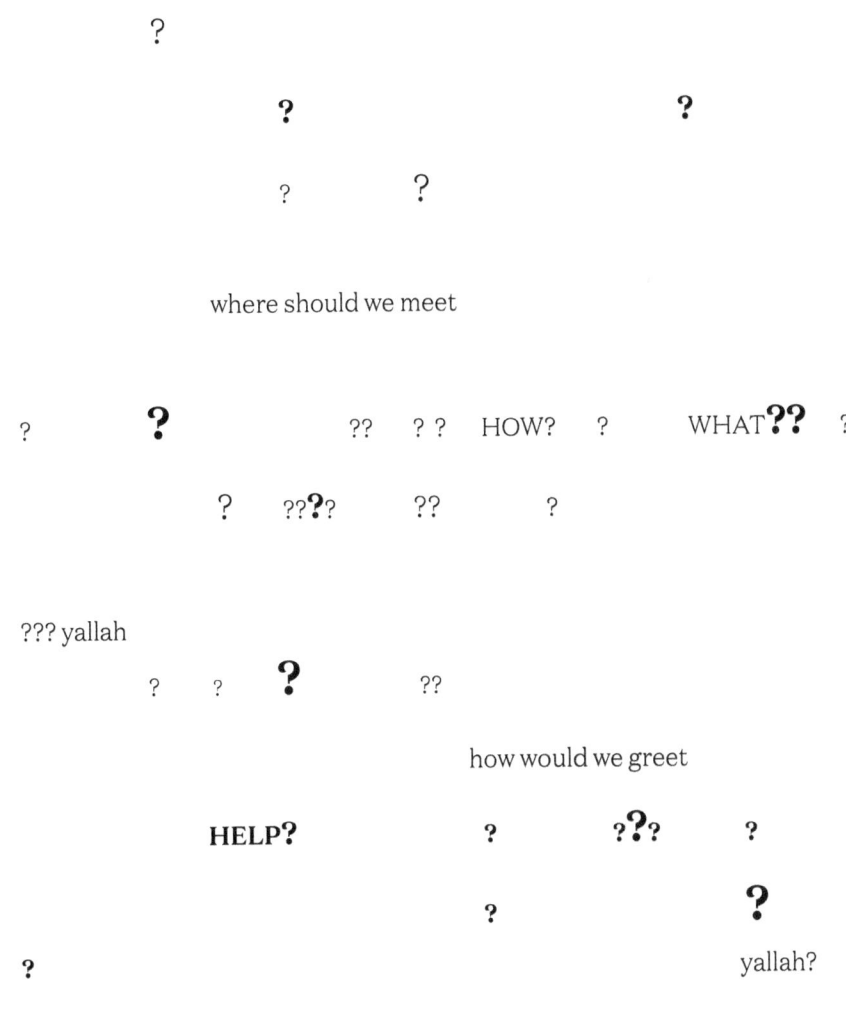

?

?   ?

?   ?

where should we meet

?   **?**   ??   ? ?   HOW?   ?   WHAT**??**   ?

?   ??**?**?   ??   ?

??? yallah

?   ?   **?**   ??

how would we greet

HELP?   ?   ?**?**?   ?

?   **?**

?   yallah?

our homes are not for strangers

take something with you, anything,

                      your cat. your mother's gold necklace. your
grandmother's diamond ring.

                 your daughter's bird blanket. your son's stuffed
elephant.   grandpa's medicine. your son's inhaler.

            water. a box of tampons. a book. your prayer shawl. your
prayer blanket.

                 a knife. a thumb drive. your   copper
coffee pot.   . hair
brush. toothbrush. toothpaste. glasses. soap.   socks. pants.
grandpa's medicine. your son's inhaler.   a

      family picture.   baby
food. biscuits. water.

                 you will not be just a
         . thumb drive.

               your husband's comb. your
daughter's medicine. a drawing by your grandfather.

           a handful of dirt.

       a piece of Syria
   hold it close.

in my arms, you'll feather

you could be my child.

I could hold you on my lap as another daughter.   paint circles on the velvet
warmth of your back.   small bone blades might sprout wings.

in this brief nest rest till your blood labnehs.   thick tangy salt. sun
sprays through the window.   dust diamonds your eyelashes.

let me look at you. stroke your neck.   help you release your throat
of lament.   imagine the wind as kind.

·

all the women in your dreams look like me

K's eyes were wild violets rinsed by rain. His laugh a ladder to the top-most floor. 23. Dark hair unruly. He thought there would be planes. To feel that pressure press before the open blue. Familiar machines. Metal's symmetry. Joint to joint. Simple. He could shoot. Killed his first squirrel at 5. Watched it fall from the tree. Fur still holding wind. Stood over it. Stroked the tail. Such softness his hands quaked. What would you do to escape? Dust settled in his father's lungs and drowned him in fiber. Bound by. Kudzu. So many children. In his dreams, wide bowls howled. K's future a golden string snaking green. He was the oldest. Joined the Marines. Strapped his gun tight. A shield. Charged the dunes. The sky black with smoke. *Like swimming in the night.* The ripe air burned his eyes. He traced the bones of my spine and sand rose to meet horizon. *Do you remember the first time you saw blue?* His hand up my neck. My silky curls. Two flames for eyes. Those days I was always burning. My uncle. My brother strip-searched at the airport. K's fingers crested my shoulders. Down my valleys. *Safe now*, he whispered. I watched the dunes shift behind his eyelids. Covered his mouth with mine. *Give me your breath.* K cupped my neck. *You. Look. Like them.* The first patrol. He jumped off the truck. A body. Unveiled. The glossy black curls. Quaking with wind. Touched her cheek. My cheek. My grandmother's cheek. My grandmother's hands of honey. My aunt's hands of blood. Nothing thick enough. To hide the children. Pebbles in a dry river. They begged the mountains. The sand. The greedy desert air. They begged everything. You have the gun, so here is my money. You have the gun, so here is my body. You have the gun, so here is my country. The sun seared his pupils blind. Where was the forest's silence?

.

The stream in spring? *Everything narrows to the people next to you.* Their heartbeats' thunder. I roll over. Spread my legs. K's eyes calm to glass. He wanted to trap the sky. Claim cloud. I cannot give more than the earth's sensation. I let him begin with taste.

ballad for the bird children of Beqaa

tents sag to mud & wind & children find ways to morning praise together—
stick rock feather. they squat the earth lost in a beetle's journey. head-turn
at wind through an empty can. the call of a bird they do not know. sitti, they
skip through starglow. legs bonethin. they sleep deep despite the din. nest
comma-curled in one bed—brother sister mother—head head head. sing prayers
to the new. memorize the maze to the toilet pit. they listen to strangers. their
haphazard flock an excuse to spit & scream. anything to forget their hollowed
bellies. wingbeats that dream a fast escape to strange lands. the stars wink
wrong in the sky. what was home becomes unknown.

we visit the beach at night to remind the waves we are alive

all was black so black
I blinked and blinked till blind

a wide retina to the sea
that answered
salt

I wasn't a fragrance
I was a piece of seasoning
Lot's wife
turned pillar
and I wanted it

darkness gave its mouth to me

your hair wet at the scalp
after an evening's vigor
the slurp slurp of love

we aren't the only ones who want to bring up
the water of the other

we aren't the only ones who wring each other out
to slake more than thirst

your desire isn't currency / you hover over map lines

                                        fake cunning—
                              you haven't eaten in a week
                                 your 4 children under 7
                                haven't eaten in a week

               where can you take them?

if someone says tributary do you think
safety? if someone says safety
do you think passage? if someone says
America?

          (*our country has blood all over the place*)

                                        which country?
                                       whose children?
                                              choose?

ya'aburnee

in pigtails. in torn sweaters. other children
ride their bikes over building bones.

sun brights their eyes. still.
though Iran. Turkey. Russia. we shake their fate like bones.

at some point the numbers (400,000 / 1 million / 1.2 million) scramble the brain
numb. I rattle my ribs with fists. jolt my bones.

stare at one 6-year-old's effort to make bike wheels turn over this terrain.
hold her face in my mind. its delicate bones.

the picture was taken yesterday. same day my daughter discovered
the bell on her bike. ring metal bones!

I bow my head. cover it. deference to all the ancestors. I whisper
God save them. give my prayer structure. mouth its bones.

sitti gets to be white as long as she's behaving

for Nina Simone

Don't silence the woman at dinner who yells her mind.

I need her. Like Nina screaming her low piano about those
girls in Mississippi. (They weren't hers. They are ours.)

Syrians crumble every border after ANOTHER! CHEMICAL! ATTACK!
(Why does it hurt so much when my child isn't the one burning?)

Mississippi. Syria. (We are them. They are ours.)
LISTEN! DO SOMETHING!

Let the soup be cold. Scream, Nina. Goddamn scream.

sitti learns the word *token*

(a broken ghazal)

First poetry gathering in Oregon, I am asked

where my veil is. Is it the zucchini dip? We are all labeled something, sitti,
thanks to our pan-Arab cousins' rage. Or, maybe, I'd be asked

which box to check regardless. America, what if I
mention my Jewish mother? She died a decade ago. She asked

if it was OK to be cremated even though she wasn't the one
who went to temple. I was. In North Carolina, as a teenager, I was asked

what church I went to—Baptist, Methodist, Christ of
something. Never a temple or mosque. That couldn't be asked.

Unsafe, somehow, what's unknown. I can grasp at understanding now
that I am grown and not embarrassed on the school bus when asked

almost any question about me. My untamable hair gave
everything away anyway, my opaque eyes, and, when asked

my skin's answer was always caramel brown to the sun's strength. I don't know
where I'm going with this. It isn't like I can return, even if asked,

to Lebanon or Syria or the Austro-Hungarian Empire before
the pogroms or Dachau or Beirut in 1982, or even, 2024. I don't want to be asked

when I was born. Now. Here. Fearmongers erect their walls.
They beat the desperate with clubs. Even in this place my ancestors asked

to escape to. The wolf grows fat with hoarding. I dream
of the breath's need for exit. My mother's neshama before she asked

for chemo. Did she ask? She was so sick by then. Her mind beaten
by unanswerable questions. Think of my daughter's first tooth. If asked

I remember her gums gave up rivers. I dream of blood. Between my legs.
Out my ears. My stomach a country split and spilling. Children asked

to be carried away from guns. Their mothers. Their fathers. Me. Wrapping them
in whatever is left. Sitti, you died before this angry world was fixed. If asked

your long arms could have cleared a path. *See the lightning*, you'd say.
Watch me bend the sky.

tell the ocean

You, who hold the cipher song of whales.
Clam cymbal and kombu semaphore. You, who
porpoise dance and orca heave. Keep your slick dark surface slick.
Midnight a kohl-eyed woman. The sun inside her pupils.

We have already lost your brother earth.

Without a home we stilt walk. Unsteady.
Unable to come down. Legs quiver. Leg shiver.
In every boat ghosts fake flesh.

Once, I floated while you cradled my head as precious fruit.

there is only so much vibration of a body
so much vibration of a body so much

======   ======   ======   ===== ===   ===   ===   ==
     =======   ========= ========= =====   =========
     ===== ======   ===== ========   ======
       ===vibration=====   ========= ===== =======
       ==========   =======   =====   ===of==== ==

     =======   ========= =======   =======   ======
       ======   ===========
                   ===========   ======== =====a==

   ======   ======   ===== == ===== ===== ===   ==   ==
                     ==== === ===   ===

   ====   ======body====   ======   ==========   ======

       ========   ================
==============   ================

   ======   ========= before
                                              ======
========== ======   === == == = = ==

       that body

     ======= ======   === sees stillness ====   ===

            as

                   the condition of not being alive

42

hearing Idlib will be bombed by three countries I try to seduce you

a rithā' for John

perhaps you should
sex me here, thicken my blood
take my milk for gall—
blame me
for my desire, as it mirrors
your desire for din
(sizzle and tiny 0s and 1s
placed beside the bed confuse)
grieve my life?—No!

MY   BODY   IS   NUMINOUS

magnificent in its multiplying multiplicity
multitudinous!
magnanimous!
mmmmmmmmmmmmmmmmmmmmmmmmmmmmmmmmmmmmmmm
(milky hole for your mounting
mole)
urbane profane
nature outwits spoiling and
we'll all be dead soon anyhow so

unroot reason—
unmake the bed—

my head needs that thing you do
from shoulder curve to neck
crown me Lady Macbeth
conductor of grief's wind
all season my hedonist reach
gave these tears to the air

                                    drown here drown there
                        octagonal bed above your swirling head
                            hail wind   rain   sun
                            hail wind   rain   sun
                            hail wind   rain   sun

                                        hide your fire
                                         so the dark
                                     may plot with time

                                           owls fly
                                      above the music
                                       bats trumpet
                                      geometric grids
                                  in a triangular rhombus

                                        thick breath
                               the only answer to sorrow
                                  if joy goes swiftly gone—

it is an old story: women's bodies as spoils

when we are as ephemeral as you—
the body less vessel than conduit—
children pulled filthy and pulped from rubble and still you
pierce my soft belly with two fingers to help me remember
what was once housed there

                                        we border cross—pelvis to pelvis—
                                            flesh surrender as good
                                                as any peace treaty

this
worship does not subsume
destruction but its after-
shocks ripple the dust we
fools create

try not to die

sitti learns her address

Don't cross the phantom line from Washington Street to where the Italians & Jews have staked out their blocks. Garlic hung in double helix. Planets of cheese. Kitchens tight as a fist. *Before this did I even exist or was I just deep green mountain breath, blown cloud?* The daughter of priests? Not Lebanon, but something before. Before the French. The English. Something where Muslims & Christians nodded to neighbors under the shadow of Mount Sannine. Ottoman. Greek. Melkite. Maronite. Muslim. The *m* in the mouth watering like a salted lemon. Zahlé. City of poets & wine.

Here buildings blaze & tremble with the Levant. Little Syria. Arab ghetto. Slum.

One brother fights the Irish boy 50 pounds larger to defend the smallest brother. His nose breaks. The other boy's nose breaks.

Always a border somewhere & those intent on crossing.

The streets heave iron. This place wants to send them back.

She misses sand.
She misses foam.

take something with you

your mother's

coffee pot.

daughter's
medicine. your son's

biscuits.   biscuits.

soap.

a backpack.   take
something with you

your
daughter's medicine.

a handful of

need.

(ssshhhhh) quiet, I'm dreaming...

a country let me dream a country let me dream a country let me
dream a country let me dream a country let me make a country
in my dream I will dream my country I will dream my country let me
dream myself into a country in my dream let me let me let me let
me make myself let me let me into let me let me let me dream into a
dream into a country that is mine so I can learn learn learn learn
learn learn learn learn how to be how to be how to be how to be to
be be be be be be be be bebe bebe be be bebe bebe bebe be be bebe
bebebebebebebebebebebebebebebebebebebebebebebe

==
================= ========== ========= ====
============== ========== ================= =======
============ ===== === ======= ============ ======
===== ====== ========

someone who reads sacred texts someone who reads missives
in order to dismiss their assumed place on earth, this tent, this dirt of
another country not my country not my dirt but still it creases the
skin sinks in to the place we're in—I didn't dream someone who adds
one Lebanese to one Syrian one Greek to one Turk to one Syrian to
one Jordanian to one Syrian to get a new someone who multiplies a
country into a country someone who adds rubble to rubble to rubble
to rubble to rubble to dust to dust to dust someone who mingles harp
drum oud bell to bomb bird thirst blue to blood to blood to blood to blood
to blood to blood to blood to blood add blood to blood to blood to blood to
blood to blood add blood add blood add blood add blood add blood add blood
and get country

terrorist

Was it the Oklahoma City bombing? No. It was my grandmothers' living rooms.
Meditations on Germany. Iran. Lebanon. Israel. From the French, *terroriste*,
1795, to take down a king. Guillotine for injustice. Or, 1920, to colonize a country.
One grandmother could name hers. *Hitler killed her*, she said fingering a photo
of my great-aunt's curls. Terrorist = fanatic, one who causes terror. But, also,
terrorist = those who seek to purge perceived difference, to create the world
in their image. Someone who, as Voltaire said, *persecutes his brother
because he is not of his opinion.*

My other grandmother would say, *fear your neighbor*. They'll lend you
milk one month. Hitch your feet to the car's bumper the next. Both
grandmothers assumed everyone who wasn't us wanted us dead.

We / you are *an impediment*. We / you *who cause alarm; dread.*
We / you *who cause panic.*

My grandmothers are dead.

I hardly leave the house now. Signs everywhere demand justice.
The word gives me hives.

When did here become here? Was it us or you who changed the flag from
symbol to spear? Are we fighters? Are we clear?

I am uncomfortable with my own face. My rage sparks daily.
For my daughter, I hug my chest. Breathe into my rapid heart.
Stop now, I say to the mirror. Stop now, terrorist.

take

                your daughter
                      your son

                       your   mother   your
sister

                        your husband

you shake your head and get something other than sea

Your mother is dead. That much is true.

The dark ooze she planted into your soft ears before she left—
no matter how you shake it won't leak out.
If you had a mirror you could search for her face in your own.
If you had a toy rabbit you could remember her soft touch.
You have neither.

You have bombs. That much is true.

She told you this would happen. But you forgot
to believe or you forgot to remember. The dark
ooze earthquakes your eardrum. When you still your skull
it dreams for you.

A thousand stories away your father
imagines lifting you and your sister
out of rubble. His palms a second earth.
He knows the dark liquid's song—
but will not join its singing.

He has amal enough for the entire battered world.

He thinks all it takes is a cigarette break

by the young man holding a missile. All it takes
is his lips to each of his children's damp foreheads.
The kiss making its mark.

That much is true.

God awake once more in the blessing of his breath.

something   anything

                        to remember

                                                        your
daughter

                stuck
                                        stuck
whatever is
stuck   is
                        you

to kill a poet first you must destroy the world

for Mohammad Bashir al-Aani

when you touch me after our daughter is born
you recall that water goes back to the sea

though I'm a stream forgotten by the clouds
the valleys of me don't plump

I'm salted, torn meat; I hang on
invisible hooks

the past dissolves in our daughter's hungry
hole; mine is barely alive

I could fake it—but that was never our story
even now as you pretend to want what's left

a friend said she gave her pussy to the second child
her clitoris cleaved and jagged

I'm a poet
I claw my way to desire

(before the war, the orange tree silenced us with its blossoms
before the war, we were three: my wife, my son...)

the poet takes whatever is left
and breathes it back alive

Notes

The epigraph is from Wanda Coleman's poem, "Amnesia Fugue" from *Mercurochrome: New Poems*, Black Sparrow Press, 2001.

Page 2—**slip of light** was inspired by the events of September 3, 2015, when Syrian refugees three-year-old Alan Kurdi, five-year-old Galip, and their mother, Rehan, were drowned near Turkey trying to reach the Greek island of Kos. Their father, Abdullah, survived. Images of his family dead on the beach circulated throughout international media.

slip of light and the poem **hearing Idlib will be bombed by three countries I try to seduce you** are my version of a rithā', a type of ancient Arabic elegiac poetry women often wrote for their partners or brothers who died in war. In this collection, both rithā's reference the sorrow of fathers who have lost members of their families. I write as a mother who empathizes with this sorrow.

Page 9—*sitti* means grandmother in the Lebanese dialect of Arabic.

Page 10—**sacrifice** refers partially to the use of Chapman Elementary School's large chimney in Portland, Oregon for the Vaux's Swifts September migration.

Page 11—*na'am* means yes in most Arabic dialects.

Page 12—**they named their child Thawra** was inspired by the story of a couple naming their child *thawra* (Arabic for revolution) in the book, *No Turning Back: Life, Loss, and Hope in Wartime Syria* by Rania Abouzeid.

Page 17—The title for **poetry should be an anti-weapon** comes from the Syrian-French poet Maram al-Masri. In late summer 2016, five-year-old Omran Daqneesh was injured in a military strike on the rebel-held Qaterji neighborhood of Aleppo, Syria. His photo became a symbol of the Syrian revolution.

Page 19—The title **and for water they drank rain** is inspired from a correspondence between poets Anne Waldman and Joanne Kyger.

The last line in **and for water they drank rain** is from a circular the municipality of Bcharre, Lebanon, distributed forbidding landlords to rent properties to displaced Syrian families and requiring the expulsion of those refugees already in residence (*The Independent*, June 22, 2018). It is also the birthplace of the famous Lebanese-American poet Kahlil Gibran. This poetic sequence owes a debt of gratitude to the Dutch bassist Wilbert de Joode for his explanation of what it feels like to improvise with a jazz group he'd been playing music with for several decades.

Page 25—*yallah* means hurry up in Arabic.

Page 31—**in my arms, you'll feather** references the drained yogurt dish common in Levantine cooking known as *labneh*.

Page 32—**all the women in your dreams look like me** is for K and other U.S. Marines traumatized by the Gulf War.

Page 34—Beqaa is a region east of Beirut, Lebanon where many Syrian refugee families have lived in tents since the Syrian civil war began in 2011.

Page 36—The line about blood in **your desire isn't currency / you hover over map lines** was said in 2016 by a first-grade girl in a Syrian refugee camp in Lebanon.

Page 37—**ya'aburnee** was written after reading this sentence from an interview of a Syrian refugee grandmother in Rania Abouzeid's book, *No Turning Back: Life, Loss, and Hope in Wartime Syria*: "Everything can be rebuilt, but we will not be able to bring our children back if they are killed."

ya'aburnee, in Arabic, means you bury me, because you love someone so much you hope to die before them so you don't have to live without them.

Page 38—the title for **sitti gets to be white as long as she's behaving** borrows and changes a line from Jess Rizkallah's poem, "if teta never had to leave Lebanon I wonder if she would make preserves." It is dedicated to Nina Simone who continues to astonish me with her bravery and brilliance. I first heard Simone's song, "Mississippi Goddam" in the 1990s when I was traveling and living in the southern United States, over 30 years after she created it in response to the four girls who were killed in a KKK bombing in Alabama in 1963. Simone proved art can ignite revolution.

Page 39—**sitti learns the word *token*** has the word *neshama*, which, in Hebrew, means the spirit, breath, or the soul—it is often used as a tender form of address to mean that someone is an important part of your life.

Page 43—**hearing Idlib will be bombed by three countries I try to seduce you** was written in conversation with William Shakespeare's *The Tragedie of Macbeth*.

Page 49—**terrorist** owes debt to Joy Katz's poem, "In My Mother's 1935 American College Dictionary."

Page 51—In the poem **you shake your head and get something other than sea** the word *amal* means hope. In late March 2015, Bashirul Shikder's wife kidnapped their children, Yusuf, then aged five, and Zahra, who was just over a year old, and took them to Syria. Since March 2019, they were assumed to be in Baghouz, Syria, the last ISIS stronghold of the war.

Page 54—**to kill a poet first you must destroy the world** was written in response to the murder of Syrian poet Mohammad Bashir al-Aani and his son, Elyas. They had returned to Syria to bury their wife/mother in March 2016 and were kidnapped and murdered by fundamentalists shortly thereafter.

This book was written in conversation with and owes gratitude to a variety of texts and music, most notably the following:

Wendy Pearlman's *We Crossed a Bridge and It Trembled: Voices from Syria*; Alia Malek's *The Home That Was Our Country: A Memoir of Syria*; Rania Abouzeid's *No Turning Back: Life, Loss, and Hope in Wartime Syria;* Kassem Eid's *My Country: A Syrian Memoir; ISIS: Inside the Army of Terror* by Hassan Hassan and Michael Weiss; *Syria Speaks: Art and Culture from the Frontline* (ed. by Malu Halasa, Zaher Omareen and Nawara Mahfoud); Ariel Burger's *Witness: Lessons from Elie Wiesel's Classroom;* James Barr's *A Line in the Sand: Britain, France and the Struggle that Shaped the Middle East* and *Setting the Desert on Fire: T.E. Lawrence and Britain's Secret War in Arabia, 1916-1918*; Victoria Lomasko's *Other Russias; Staying Alive* by Laura Sims; Yuseef Lateef's

"Nubian Lady;" Sun Ra and His Myth Science Arkestra's "Angels and Demons at Play" and "Cosmic Tones for Mental Therapy;" Pharaoh Sanders' *Journey to the One* and *Elevation*; Kendrick Lamar's *DAMN.*; "The fear and loathing of Syrian refugees in Lebanon," October 2017 from *Al Jazeera*; "On Refugees" by Georg Diez; Dean Young's *The Art of Recklessness: Poetry as Assertive Force and Contradiction*; William Shakespeare's *The Tragedie of Macbeth*.

Acknowledgments

Several poems in this book have been reimagined as companion soundscapes on the Portland, Oregon label THRUM Recordings and can be heard at: thrumrecordings.bandcamp.com

Deep thanks to the editors of the following presses where various versions of this book was recognized as a finalist or semi-finalist: River River Books, YesYes Books, and Milk & Cake Press.

And thank you to the 2019 Creative Capital selection committee for semi-finalist recognition of portions of this manuscript and musical compositions by my duo, Thick In The Throat Honey.

And, also, many thanks to the editors and organizers of the following journals and festivals where versions of the poems below first appeared or were performed:

Nimrod International Journal: "slip of light"

1001: "sitti learns the word *cat*"

About Place Journal: "in my arms, you'll feather," "ballad for the bird children of Beqaa," "all the women in your dreams look like me," "to kill a poet first you must destroy the world," "terrorist," and "sitti teaches me Arabic as pastry" (nominated for a Pushcart 2021)

clade song 9: "tell the ocean"

Hawai'i Review: "sacrifice"

Queen Mob's Teahouse: "and for water they drank rain"

Sunflowers at Midnight: "you shake your head and get something other than sea"

VoiceCatcher and *Calyx: A Journal of Art and Literature* (reprinted for anniversary issue): "my daughter discovers synchronicity"

Unchaste Anthology Vol. III: "sitti gets to be white as long as she's behaving"

"ballad for the bird children of Beqaa," "and for water they drank rain," and "poetry should be an anti-weapon" were all featured as part of Daniel Brandes' composition "other echoes inhabit the garden: for tenor and gated tape," performed with saxophonist John C. Savage at *The Extradition Series*, October 20, 2018, Leaven Community Church, Portland, Oregon.

"on hearing Idlib will be bombed by three countries I try to seduce you" was reimagined as a soundscape with saxophone and flute by John C. Savage as part of the *Be About Love Festival* at the Blackfish Gallery, Portland, Oregon, October 2020.

A version of "and for water they drank rain" was part of a performance by Thick In The Throat Honey (with saxophonist John C. Savage and dancer Kayla Banks) for Fused Creative's *The Feminine Era*, April 27, 2019, in Portland, Oregon. Special thanks to Meg Nanna and Jessica Green for vision, support, and belief in art. You are soul sisters.

Several poems in this collection were repurposed as part of a performance with Thick In The Throat Honey based on Khadijah Queen's poetic line: "I heard a howling but did not run" on the downtown streets of Portland, Oregon for Risk/Reward's Pavement: A Festival of Pop-up Performances in Public Spaces, August 2, 2018. *Shukran* to organizer, curator, and friend Tracy Cameron Francis for encouraging us to be loud! Louder!

Several poems in this collection were reimagined with improvisation, electronics, and movement as part of Performance Works Northwest workshop #2, curated by Stephanie Lavon Trotter, September 28, 2024. Thank you to Stephanie and Linda Austin for the support, space, warm audience, and chance for dreaming.

Gratitude to *ANMLY* literary magazine for publishing my interview series on Arab American poets: "Witness the Hour: Conversations with Arab American Poets Across the Diaspora," where many conversations that contributed to the creation of this book began.

Gratitude also to *Poetry Northwest* for publishing my essay, "Repair," about the complexity and impact of the wars and politics of the past decades on the Arab American poetic diaspora, specifically mothers.

A deep bow to the Black Earth Institute for their fellowship (2018-2021), The Mineral School Residency (now MARS), and Sou'wester Artist Residency for the time and support needed to complete this manuscript.

A million blown kisses to poet and activist, Mohja Kohf, for her tireless work helping Syrian refugees, her kind explanations about the beginning of the protest movement and leading me down many paths to understanding the history of the conflict in the region and my own family's history more clearly.

Hugs to all the poets I taught and collaborated with in my living room about the role of the poet in the world. I cannot thank you enough for your brilliance and open hearts, most especially Vivienne Popperl, Phil

Meehan, Kris Demien, Armin Tolentino, Suzanne LaGrande, John Miller, Suzy Harris, Rebecca Lynne Bluemel, Katie Sharrow Nichols, Cynthia McGean, and Lezlie Amara Piper. You've restored my faith.

To Black Earth Institute fellows Lauren Camp, Jacqueline Johnson, Alexis Lathem, Petra Kuppers, Amanda Ngoho Reavey, Austin Smith, and DJ Lee, who told me to keep going. Encouragement is no small thing.

So much gratitude to my First Matter Press family—the fantastic editors (ash good, Lauren Paredes, Hailey Spencer, and Emily Moon) and readers (Sonya Wohletz and Andra Vltavín) for their shrewd, caring suggestions on my work, gentle handling of my special needs, and brilliance; the cover artist Pearlyn Tan for her heart-breaking, stunning cover art; and, my cheering, daring, brilliantly supportive cohort: Annemarie Eayrs, Violeta Garza, and nawa angel a.h.. I would never have gotten here without you.

And, as always, to my husband and daughter, for listening to dozens of versions of these poems, making me meals, remembering to feed the cat, and granting me deep patience while this book was being written. In every way, you are my life.

PHOTO: YAARA VALEY

CLAUDIA SALEEBY SAVAGE is a poet, essayist, and disabled mama whose writing and performance explores diaspora and the landscape of the body. She is the author of *metal used for beauty alone* (The Poetry Box for print + voice), *Bruising Continents* (Spuyten Duyvil), and *The Last One Eaten: A Maligned Vegetable's History* (Finishing Line Press), with recent work in *Poetry Northwest*, *Nimrod*, *About Place*, and *River Teeth*. Saleeby Savage has received support from many organizations including RACC, Ucross, Jentel, The Black Earth Institute, MARS, and the Atlantic Center for the Arts. She creates alone and with her music-text duo Thick In The Throat Honey (they were 2019 semi-finalists for a Creative Capital award on the Syrian refugee crisis). She works in the field of renewable energy and lives with her experimental jazz musician husband, daughter, and vocal cat in the Pacific Northwest.

2025

FEATURED ARTIST PEARLYN TAN

WALING WALING PALPITATIONS
nawa angel a.h.

THE DYING ROOM
RECIPIENT OF THE PRIMA MATERIA AWARD
annemarie eayrs

BRAVA
violeta garza

FIRST YOU MUST DESTROY THE WORLD
claudia saleeby savage

2024

FEATURED ARTIST ALEXANDRA STRENFEL

GREENHOUSE
sophie hall

SUSPENDED IN MY INSECTICIDE JAR
clara mcauley

2023

FEATURED ARTIST LARA ROUSE

FLOATING BONES
rae diamond

TEN-CENT FLOWER & OTHER TERRITORIES
charity e. yoro

OUR FAVORITE PEOPLE IN THE ROOM
edited by ash good, lauren paredes & emily moon

2022

FEATURED ARTIST RACHEL MULDER

BETWEEN THESE BORDERS WANDERS A GOLEM
ahuva s. zaslavsky

EVEN THE AIR, TOO HEAVY
riley danvers

ONE ROW AFTER / BIR SIRA SONRA
sonya wohletz

SOMEONE I CAN HOLD GENTLY
xylophone mykland

STORIES FOR WHEN THE WOLVES ARRIVE
hailey spencer

2021

2020

2019

2018

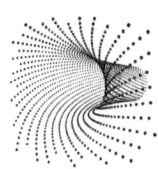

FIRSTMATTERPRESS
Portland, Ore.